TRADITIONAL JAZZ SERIES

CHICAGO-STYLE JAM SESSION

TENOR SAXOPHONE

By Raymond Hubbe
& John Golden

4218

MUSIC MINUS ONE

4218

TRADITIONAL JAZZ SERIES

CHICAGO-STYLE JAM SESSION

DISC "A" COMPLETE VERSION TRACK	DISC "A" MINUS VERSION TRACK	DISC "B" SLOW-TEMPO PRACTICE TRACK		PAGE	CONCERT LEADSHEET
			About this Recording 4		
	9	1	Tuning note		
1	10	2	Rosetta 6		22
2	11	3	'Deed I Do 8		23
3	12	4	Blues My Naughty Sweetie Gives to Me............. 10		24
4	13	5	Sugar 12		25
5	14	6	Darktown Strutters' Ball 14		26
6	15	7	Royal Garden Blues 16		27
7	16	8	Poor Butterfly... 18		28
8	17	9	That's a Plenty 20		29
			Credits & Musician Info 30		

ABOUT THIS RECORDING

THE MUSIC MINUS ONE TRADITIONAL JAZZ SERIES has been carefully conceived to address key elements of performance in early jazz styles. There are many offshoots of New Orleans jazz that make up a broad continuum of divergent styles from Ragtime to Mainstream. Such labels are important for identification only and their use is to encourage creativity through stylistic integrity.

This volume, *Chicago-Style Jam Session,* emphasizes collectively improvised ensembles and the succession of individual solos. These generally unstructured ensembles are a key element of this freewheeling style. The rhythmic texture is rooted in the swing feel of the late 1930s, and the instrumentation is typical of the New York groups of this genre. The songs are popular melodies from the 1900s to 1930s as well as multithematic compositions and blues.

Sometimes this style is referred to as the New York-Chicago style, sometimes as post-Chicago style. It has also been called "Nicksieland," a play on "Dixieland" that recognizes a Greenwich Village nightclub called "Nick's," where this music was showcased in the 1950s. Chicago-style jazz is named for the city where it first developed. In the 1920s, many New Orleans musicians, including Joe "King" Oliver, Jimmy Noone, Johnny and "Baby" Dodds, Freddie Keppard, "Jelly Roll" Morton, Louis Armstrong, the Original Dixieland Jazz Band, and the New Orleans Rhythm Kings actively performed and recorded in Chicago. There are also many younger musicians around Chicago who were profoundly influenced by their music, including Eddie Condon, Benny Goodman, Gene Krupa, Muggsy Spanier, Bud Freeman and many others. By the 1930s many of these same musicians moved on to New York. Some continued to perform in the New Orleans tradition and others became significant figures of the Swing era. As the Big Band era closed, improvising soloists still found work in New York clubs such as Nick's, Eddie Condon's and the Metropole. The texture was distinctly in the New Orleans tradition but the language was Swing and directly reflected the synthesis that took place in Chicago.

The musicians chosen for this session are, in a way, exponents of this tradition. Their personal styles are amalgamations of the greatest stylists who preceded them. You can hear in Hal Smith aural glimpses of Dave Tough and George Wettling. You can hear in Jon-Erik shades of Muggsy Spanier and Wild Bill Davison. Brian Ogilvie's voice of choice is flavored by the sonorities of Bud Freeman and Eddie Miller, and I myself owe more than a little bit to Edmond Hall's style. The other musicians were chosen for these qualities as well, and as a result, this stylistically accurate recording demonstrates the inner workings of collective improvisation in a traditional jazz context.

THE SONGS:

ROSETTA: This 1933 composition by stride pianist Earl "Fatha" Hines has long been a popular jam session standard.

'DEED I DO: From 1926, this is another well-worn standard that really swings.

BLUES (MY NAUGHTY SWEETIE GIVES TO ME): This was composed in 1919 and is not actually a blues as the title might imply. Many publishers did this to capitalize on the "blues" craze.

SUGAR: This was a 1926 hit by Maceo Pinkard and popularized by singers including Billie Holiday and Bessie Smith.

THE DARKTOWN STRUTTER'S BALL: A unique 20-bar form. This popular song, from 1917, is still very much a traditional jazz standard. The composer, Shelton Brooks, is also known for "Some of These Days" and "Walkin' the Dog".

ROYAL GARDEN BLUES: The Williams brothers had their own publishing company in Chicago and wrote this in 1919. It is a multi-theme composition with a built-in modulation. Named after a Chicago dance hall, it is an interesting treatment of the 12-bar blues form.

POOR BUTTERFLY: This classic ballad was composed in 1916. The melody and harmonies are wonderfully sophisticated and unique. Although in general we endeavored to stay true to the original, this recording has implemented a few chord changes that reflect the way the song is generally performed.

THAT'S A PLENTY: From 1914, this is a classic "warhorse" of the genre. It is a multi-theme composition with a 16-bar chorus. The full band performance reflects the typical harmony parts that are derived from the original orchestration.

HOW TO USE THIS RECORDING

Listen carefully to hear how the parts weave together. Use the melody cues and chord symbols to guide your harmonies and find the most logical places to add your voice to the texture. Remember: collective improvisation is not everyone making a solo simultaneously. The role of the instruments in the ensemble passages is to provide melodic and rhythmic counterpoint to the lead voice while emphasizing pivotal harmonic relationships. Essentially, you are spontaneously creating an orchestration. Precise ensemble figures have been avoided to provide soloists with maximum freedom and to stay true to the Chicago style. Great care has been taken to optimize the potential development of many important skills: melodic interpretation and embellishment, collective improvisation in a typical "front line," solo improvisation with a swing rhythm section, leadsheet reading skills, sight transposition, and using and following head arrangements. Besides instrument specific arrangements, this book includes concert leadsheets for all of the songs with a "roadmap." This is a reflection of the professional standard for performance in this idiom, since it is generally unwritten. Challenge yourself first by learning the songs and then by using the leadsheet roadmaps as if the bandleader is telling you the arrangement off the top of his/her head.

The "B" disc in this package contains a special slow-tempo version of each piece which can be used as you get yourself "up to speed," and which may help you as you experiment with your own improvisations.

TENOR SAX

Rosetta

by Earl Hines

'Deed I Do

by Walter Hirsch
& Fred Rose

TENOR SAX

Blues
(My Naughty Sweetie Gives to Me)

by Swanstone,
McCarron & Morgan

TENOR SAX

Sugar
(That Sugar Baby o'Mine)

by Maceo Pinkard, Edna B. Pinkard
and Sidney D. Mitchell

MMO 4218

The Darktown Strutters' Ball

by Shelton Brooks

MMO 4218

Royal Garden Blues

TENOR SAX

by Clarence & Spencer Williams

Poor Butterfly

by John Golden
& Raymond Hubbell

That's A Plenty

by Ray Gilbert
& Lew Pollack

Concert Lead Sheet

Rosetta

4 Bar Piano Intro
Solo Lead
Ens. Tpt. Lead
Open Solos (3X)
Ens. Tpt. Lead
4-Bar Drum Tag, 4 Bar Ens. Tag

by Earl Hines
& William Henri Wood

'Deed I Do

8 Bar Piano Intro
Solo Melody
Ensemble (Tpt. Lead)
Open Solos (3X on CD)
Ensemble Out Chorus (Tpt. Lead)
Bass Solo on Bridge

By Walter Hirsch
& Fred Rose

MMO 4218

Blues
(My Naughty Sweetie Gives to Me)

Last 8 Ens. Intro
Solo Melody 8, Ens. 8, Solo 8, Ens. 8
Ensemble (Tpt Lead)
Open Solos (2x on CD)
Trade 4's (1x)
Ensemble Out Chorus (Tpt Lead)
    4 Bar Drum Tag, Last 8 Ens. w/Double Ending

by Swanstone,
McCarron
& Morgan

Sugar
(That Sugar Baby o'Mine)

4 Bar Piano Intro
1X Solo Lead, 1X Ens. Tpt Lead
Open Solos 1 1/2 X
Ens. Tpt. Lead From Bridge Out

by Maceo Pinkard, Edna B. Pinkard
& Sidney D. Mitchell

MMO 4218

The Darktown Strutters' Ball

LAST 8 ENS. W/SOLO BREAKS
ENSEMBLE (TPT LEAD)
OPEN SOLOS (3X)
SOFT ENS.
ENSEMBLE OUT CHORUS (TPT LEAD)
    TAG LAST 8 3X W/BREAKS (BONE, CLAR, TPT, TENOR, DRUMS)

by Shelton Brooks

Royal Garden Blues

Ens. Intro
2X Verse [A] 2X Break Strain [B]
4 Bar Modulation [C]
2x Chorus, Open Solos (8x) [D]
Out Choruses (3x) [D]
4 Bar Drum Tag, 4 Bar Ens Tag

by Clarence & Spencer Williams

MMO 4218

Poor Butterfly

Last 8 Guitar Intro
Solo Melody
Open Solo Chorus
1/2 Chorus Ens. Tpt Lead
Solo Lead (8 bars)
Ens. Tpt Lead Last 8 w/ritard

by John Golden
& Raymond Hubbell

That's A Plenty

ENS. TPT. LEAD [A] [B] [A] (SLIGHT VARIATION)
ENS. CHORUS [C]
INTERLUDE (DOGFIGHT) [D]
OPEN SOLOS [C]   (8X ON CD)
DOGFIGHT [D]
ENS. OUT CHORUSES [C]   (3X ON CD)
4 BAR DRUM TAG, 4 BAR ENS. TAG

by Ray Gilbert
& Lew Pollack

THE MUSICIANS

BRIAN OGILVIE (tenor saxophone)

After a three-year stint in the mid-1990s with the renowned Jim Cullum Jazz Band of San Antonio, Texas, this Vancouver, Canada native moved to New Orleans. A hard-swinging virtuoso on saxophone and clarinet, Brian has worked and recorded with jazz legends including Joe Williams, Harry "Sweets" Edison, and Dick Hyman. Work as a featured soloist in the company of mainstream stalwarts such as Dan Barrett and Harry Allen find him touring regularly in Europe and in the U.S. "For You," an Arbors release under his own name, and countless others as a sideman, document his passion and enthusiasm for early jazz styles.

EVAN CHRISTOPHER (clarinet and leader)

Permanently based in New Orleans, Evan Christopher has established himself as one of the most spirited proponents of the traditional-jazz clarinet styles. His studies, which began at age 11, earned him the Louis Armstrong Jazz Award as a teen, and after university studies in Southern California he moved to New Orleans. His activities included a broad variety of work with traditional jazz musicians including Al Hirt, Lars Edegran, and veterans of Preservation Hall. In 1996, he joined Jim Cullum's Jazz Band in San Antonio, Texas for a stint that lasted just over two years and included appearances with musical guests including Dick Hyman and William Warfield. Currently, various recording projects, a busy international touring schedule, and research on the Creole clarinet style are all endeavors that show his commitment to creative music rooted in early jazz.

JON-ERIK KELLSO (trumpet)

Raised in Detroit, Jon-Erik began his craft at age 11. His love for early jazz styles found him at 17 featured alongside Wild Bill Davidson and a member of James Dapogny's Chicago Jazz Band in the late 1980s. In 1989 he moved to New York City to join Vince Giordano's Nighthawks and was quickly welcomed into mainstream and traditional jazz circles. Credits include performances and recordings with jazz veterans including Ralph Sutton, Kenny Davern, Milt Hinton, Dick Hyman, and Doc Cheatham. Keeping the tradition alive, Two Arbors Records releases showcase his talents as a leader, and work with "nouveau swing" divas such as Peggy Cone and Ingrid Lucia have gained him recognition as one of the best swing trumpet soloists on the jazz scene.

MIKE PITTSLEY (trombone)

A California native, Mike spent just over 20 years with the Jim Cullum Jazz Band. The versatility and high standard of this renowned traditional jazz band gave Mike the opportunity to really hone his craft, and the nationally syndicated radio program "Riverwalk" has showcased Mike on over 110 shows. Backing artists such as Benny Carter, Joe Williams, Dick Hyman, Lionel Hampton, and countless others are among his career highlights. In this genre, Mike considers trombonist Abram "Abe" Lincoln to be his greatest influence. To honor his mentor, Mike recorded this entire MMO session on Abe's 1930s vintage Bach trombone. This very horn can be heard on all of Abe's sessions from the 1950s with the Rampart St. Paraders as well as the Chicago-style paradigm recording "Coast Concert" with Bobby Hackett and Jack Teagarden.

JEFF BARNHART (piano)

A versatile pianist and entertainer, Jeff is an enthusiastic performer devoted to showcasing early jazz piano styles. Ragtime, boogie, stride and swing are his specialties and he keeps them fresh and vital through work as a soloist, educator, and recording artist. Recordings on Jeff's own label, Jazz Alive Records, represent a sizable catalog of his work, and concert appearances as a soloist as well as with swing and traditional-jazz festival bands find him enjoying a busy touring schedule in both the U.S. and the U.K. Jeff got hooked on the traditional jazz sound early when he heard Eddie Condon's recording, "That Toddlin' Town" and cites Jess Stacey and Earl Hines as two very strong influences for this style.

BILL HUNTINGTON (guitar)

Born in New Orleans in 1937, Bill Huntington is in many ways the quintessential New Orleans artist. Bill's first instrument at the age of 12 was banjo, which he studied with Lawrence Marrero. He switched to guitar at 16 and later to string bass. His deep roots in early jazz have kept him in great demand. Credits include recordings with many traditional jazz legends, among them Percy Humphrey, Pete Fountain, Al Hirt, Raymond Burke, Doc Cheatham and Bucky Pizzarelli. Bill can be heard regularly with Ellis Marsalis and is also active in jazz education both locally at the University of New Orleans and as a clinician in the U.S. and abroad.

JIM SINGLETON (bass)

Bassist James Singleton, one of the busiest in New Orleans, is a conduit of pure energy whose solid rhythmic concept and intuitive stylistic adaptability is the foundation of any group in which he performs. He has appeared with swing and traditional greats Clarence "Gatemouth" Brown, Lionel Hampton, and Arnette Cobb as well as many modern jazz musicians such as John Abercrombie, John Scofield, Art Baron, Ellis Marsalis, and Eddie Harris. His extensive recording credits include work with Chet Baker, Alvin "Red" Tyler, and James Booker and his own groups "3 Now 4" and "Astral Project."

HAL SMITH (drums)

Hal's passion for the early styles of jazz, of course, is evident in his swinging performances and recordings, but also in his tireless efforts as a journalist for publications such as the Mississippi Rag, as a producer of recordings by artists including Lu Watters and Ben Pollack, and as an educator for traditional jazz projects such as the AFCDJS Traditional Jazz Camp. Based near San Diego, California, Hal has established himself as an integral part of the West-Coast traditional jazz scene but frequently travels for work as a soloist, recording artist, and bandleader. Associations include appearances and recordings with Bob Wilber, Kenny Davern, Ed Polcer, Wild Bill Davison, Ralph Sutton, and Doc Cheatham. His drumming style is an encyclopedic amalgam of his favorites, among them "Baby" Dodds, George Wettling, Paul Barbarin, Gene Krupa, Sid Catlett, Nick Fatool, Zutty Singleton, Dave Tough and Ben Pollack.

Photos: Irv Kratka

MUSIC MINUS ONE

50 Executive Boulevard
Elmsford, New York 10523-1325
800-669-7464 (U.S.)/914-592-1188 (International)

www.musicminusone.com
e-mail: mmogroup@musicminusone.com

MUSIC MINUS ONE

Participation Recordings for All Instrumentalists & Singers

2002

Index

Alto Saxophone, Banjo, Baritone Saxophone, Bassoon	3
Clarinet, Double Bass	4
Drums, Equipment, Flute	5
Flute, French Horn	6
Guitar, Harp, Instructional, Oboe, Piano	7
Piano	8
Piano, Recorder, Soprano Saxophone, Tenor Saxophone, Trombone	9
Trumpet, Tuba/Bass Trombone, Vibes, Viola	10
Violin	11
Violin, Violoncello, Vocal, Vocal Alto	12
Vocal Bass-Baritone, Contralto, Mezzo-Soprano, Soprano, Tenor	13
Broadway	14
Broadway	15

About Music Minus One

Begun in 1950, MMO this year enters its 52nd year of continuous activity under the guidance of a single individual still active in guiding its programs. It has become an established part of the musician's world known to three generations of musicians, many still clients. Its catalog offers 700 titles on compact disc, with new recordings being added all the time.

MMO recordings provide musicians with a unique way to study, rehearse and perform with professional ensembles in the comfort of their own home. All types of music from jazz to chamber music as well as orchestral concerti are offered for all instruments. In recent years, the recordings have been augmented by adding professional soloists to each production. The user can now hear the solo part and then perform it themselves.

Everyone may now share the unique experience of having an ensemble at their disposal. Whether it be a thrilling symphony orchestra or a top-notch jazz rhythm section, MMO gives every musician the chance to perform with professional ensembles in their own living room.

Repertoire and Artists without Equal

MMO's repertoire is an amazing one: offering hundreds of albums ranging from classical baroque to 20th century modern, from vocal standards and jazz trios to rock-drumming and classical percussion primers, from Vivaldi's *Four Seasons* to Glazunov's 1934 *Saxophone Concerto,* from its inaugural 1950 recording of the Schubert *Trout Quintet* to its new ground-breaking *Opera with Orchestra* series, truly all-encompassing.

Superior Quality

All of MMO's latest releases feature newly engraved printed scores, on beautiful acid-free ivory paper, often in unique and authoritative, definitive editions with annotations and performance suggestions from world-class artists. Historical liner notes and biographical information on the composers and works add an extra dimension, allowing the soloist to gain insight into each work's genesis and history.

Unrivaled Convenience

Music Minus One editions offer limitless possibilities for practice, for developing artistry and technique. World-quality soloists and orchestras, new and definitive printed editions of classic works, and innovative technologies combine to make a product without rival, one that today's musicians can utilize to the fullest.

Music Minus One • 50 Executive Boulevard • Elmsford, New York 10523-1325
Visit our two websites: www.musicminusone.com and www.pocketsongs.com

Alto Saxophone

2+2=5: A Study in Odd Times ....MMO CD 2041
Advanced Contest Solos, vol. I ....MMO CD 4115
Advanced Contest Solos, vol. II ....MMO CD 4116
Advanced Contest Solos, vol. III ....MMO CD 4117
Advanced Contest Solos, vol. IV ....MMO CD 4118
Alto Saxophone Solos: Student Edition, vol. I ....MMO CD 4101
Alto Saxophone Solos: Student Edition, vol. II ....MMO CD 4102
Band Aids for Alto Sax:
Concert Band Favorites with Orchestra ....MMO CD 4127
Beginning Contest Solos, vol. I ....MMO CD 4111
Beginning Contest Solos, vol. II ....MMO CD 4112
Classic Themes: Student Editions, 27 Easy Songs (2nd-3rd year) ....MMO CD 4130
Days of Wine & Roses/Sensual Sax: The Bob Wilber All-Stars ....MMO CD 4121
Easy Jazz Duets for Two Alto Saxophones and Rhythm Section...............MMO CD 4103
For Saxes Only: Arranged by Bob Wilber,
for alto, tenor, baritone sax, trumpet or clarinet ....MMO CD 4104
GLAZUNOV Saxophone Concerto in E-flat major,
op.109; VON KOCH Saxophone Concerto ....MMO CD 4132
Intermediate Contest Solos, vol. I ....MMO CD 4113
Intermediate Contest Solos, vol. II ....MMO CD 4114
JOBIM Brazilian Bossa Novas with Strings ....MMO CD 4106
Music for Saxophone Quartet..MMO CD 4128
Play Lead in a Sax Section: The Bob Wilber All-Stars ....MMO CD 4120
Popular Concert Favorites with Orchestra ....MMO CD 4126
Stompin' & Struttin' the New Swing:
Six Bands on a Hot Tin Roof ....MMO CD 4108
Teacher's Partner: Basic Studies for Alto Sax, first year ....MMO CD 4119
Twenty Dixieland Classics..MMO CD 4124
Twenty Rhythm Backgrounds to Standards ....MMO CD 4125
World Favorites: Student Editions,
41 Easy Selections (1st-2nd year) ....MMO CD 4129

Banjo

Bluegrass Banjo: Classic & Favorite Banjo Pieces ....MMO CD 4401
How to Play the Five-String Banjo
The Dick Weissman Method, vol. I ....MMO CD 4402
How to Play the Five-String Banjo
The Dick Weissman Method, vol. II ....MMO CD 4403

Baritone Saxophone

Music for Saxophone Quartet..MMO CD 4901
Stompin' & Struttin' the New Swing: Six Bands on a Hot Tin Roof ....MMO CD 4902

Bassoon

BEETHOVEN Quintet for Piano and Winds in E-flat major, op. 16 ....MMO CD 4605
The Joy of Woodwind Quintets ....MMO CD 4603
Masterpieces for Woodwind Quintet ....MMO CD 4602
MOZART Quintet for Piano and Winds in E-flat major, KV452 ....MMO CD 4606
Solos For The Bassoon ....MMO CD 4601
STRAVINSKY L'Histoire du Soldat (septet) ....MMO CD 4604
VIVALDI Bassoon Concerto in E minor, F.VIII, no.6 (RV484);
Bassoon Concerto in C major, F.VIII, no.17 (RV472) ....MMO CD 4607

Contents to these albums may be seen on our website at: www.musicminusone.com

Clarinet

Advanced Contest Solos, vol. I ....MMO CD 3225
Advanced Contest Solos, vol. II ....MMO CD 3226
Advanced Contest Solos, vol. III ....MMO CD 3228
Advanced Contest Solos, vol. IV ....MMO CD 3229
The Art of the Clarinet:
Baermann Method, op. 64 (4 CD Set) ....MMO CD 3241
Art Of The Solo Clarinet:
Orchestral Excerpts ....MMO CD 3206
Band Aids: Concert Band Favorites
with Orchestra ....MMO CD 3243
BEETHOVEN Quintet for Piano and Winds
in E-flat major, op. 16 ....MMO CD 3235
Beginning Contest Solos, vol. I ....MMO CD 3221
Beginning Contest Solos, vol. II.....................MMO CD 3222
BRAHMS Clarinet Quintet in B minor, op. 115
(Digitally Remastered Version) ....MMO CD 3230
BRAHMS Sonata in F minor, op. 120, no. 1;
Sonata in E-flat major, op. 120, no. 2 ....MMO CD 3208
Classic Themes: Student Editions,
27 Easy Songs (2nd-4th year) ....MMO CD 3245
Easy Clarinet Solos, vol. I - Student Level ......MMO CD 3211
Easy Clarinet Solos, vol. II - Student Level ....MMO CD 3212
Easy Jazz Duets for Two Clarinets
and Rhythm Section.....................................MMO CD 3213
First Chair Clarinet Solos:
Orchestral Excerpts ....MMO CD 3205
From Dixie to Swing.....................................MMO CD 3234
HAJDU Jewish Rhapsody for Clarinet,
Bass Clarinet and Orchestra ....MMO CD 3246
In a League of His Own: Popular Songs
played by Ron Odrich and You ....MMO CD 3215
Intermediate Contest Solos, vol. I ....MMO CD 3223
Intermediate Contest Solos, vol. II ....MMO CD 3224
Intermediate Contest Solos, vol. III................MMO CD 3227
Jazz Standards
with Rhythm Section (2 CD Set) ....MMO CD 3218
Jazz Standards with Strings (2 CD Set) ....MMO CD 3219
Jewels for Woodwind Quintet ....MMO CD 3232
Masterpieces for Woodwind Quintet ....MMO CD 3233
MOZART Clarinet Concerto in A major, KV622 (2 CD Set)
includes Bb version ....MMO CD 3238
MOZART Quintet for Piano and
Winds in E-flat major, KV452........................MMO CD 3236
MOZART Quintet in A major, KV581 (2 CD Set)
includes Bb version ....MMO CD 3207

Popular Concert Favorites with Orchestra ....MMO CD 3242
Ron Odrich Plays Standards plus You ....MMO CD 3220
SCHUMANN Phantasiestücke, op. 73;
3 Romanzen (3 Romances), op. 94 ....MMO CD 3210
Sinatra Set to Music: Kern, Weill,
Gershwin, Howard and You...........................MMO CD 3216
SPOHR Clarinet Concerto No. 1
in C minor, op. 26 ....MMO CD 3203
Stompin' & Struttin' the New Swing:
Six Bands on a Hot Tin Roof ....MMO CD 3237
STRAVINSKY L'Histoire du Soldat (septet)......MMO CD 3217
Teacher's Partner: Basic Clarinet Studies ......MMO CD 3231
The Virtuoso Clarinetist: Baermann Method,
op. 63 (4 CD Set) ....MMO CD 3240
Visions: The Clarinet Artistry
of Ron Odrich (2CD Set) ....MMO CD 3214
WEBER Clarinet Concertino, op. 26, J109;
BEETHOVEN Piano Trio No. 4,
'Street Song,' op. 11.....................................MMO CD 3204
WEBER Clarinet Concerto No. 1 in F minor, op. 73;
STAMITZ Clarinet Concerto
No. 3 in B-flat major ....MMO CD 3202
WEBER Grand Duo Concertant;
WAGNER Adagio ....MMO CD 3209
World Favorites: Student Editions,
41 Easy Selections (1st-3rd year) ....MMO CD 3244

Double Bass

2+2=5: A Study in Odd Times ....MMO CD 2047
The Beat Goes On: Jazz -
Funk, Latin, Pop-Rock ....MMO CD 4304
Beginning to Intermediate Contest Solos ......MMO CD 4301
BOTTESINI Concerto in B minor for Double Bass &
Orchestra; Grande Allegro di Concerto
for Double Bass & Orchestra.........................MMO CD 4308
For Bassists Only: Jazz Trios, Quartets,
Quintets (Ken Smith) ....MMO CD 4303
From Dixie to Swing.....................................MMO CD 4305
Intermediate to Advanced Contest Solos ......MMO CD 4302
SCHUBERT Piano Quintet in A major, op. 114, D667
'Forellen-Quintett' or 'Trout Quintet' ....MMO CD 4307
STRAVINSKY L'Histoire du Soldat (septet)......MMO CD 4306

Drums

Classical Percussion (2 CD Set)	MMO CD 5009
Drum Pad Stick Skin: Jazz play-alongs with small groups	MMO CD 5006
Drum Star Jazz Combos: Trios/Quartets/Quintets Minus You	MMO CD 5005
Eight Men in Search of a Drummer	MMO CD 5010
Fabulous Sounds of Rock Drums: A Method for the Beginner	MMO CD 5012
For Drummers Only: Jazz Band Music Minus One Drummer	MMO CD 5002
From Dixie to Swing	MMO CD 5011
Jump, Jive and Wail: 6 Swing Bands on a Hot Tin Roof	MMO CD 5007
Modern Jazz Drumming (2 CD Set)	MMO CD 5001
Open Session with the Greg Burrows Quintet (2 CD Set)	MMO CD 5013
Sit-in with Jim Chapin	MMO CD 5004
STRAVINSKY L'Histoire du Soldat (septet)	MMO CD 5014
Wipe-Out	MMO CD 5003

Equipment

Superscope PSD230 Portable Variable-Speed & Pitch CD Player*	MMO EQ 10231
Superscope Wrist/neck/clip Mini-remote for PSD230	MMO EQ 10240
Superscope FT200 Foot Pedal for PSD230 CD player	MMO EQ 10241

* See back cover for details

Flute

Advanced Contest Solos, vol. I	MMO CD 3325
Advanced Contest Solos, vol. II	MMO CD 3326
Advanced Contest Solos, vol. III	MMO CD 3328
Advanced Contest Solos, vol. IV	MMO CD 3329
Advanced Contest Solos, vol. V	MMO CD 3332
J.S. BACH Brandenburg Concerti Nos. 4 in G major (BWV1048) & 5 in D major (BWV1050)	MMO CD 3310
J.S. BACH Brandenburg Concerto No. 2 in F major; HAYDN Flute Concerto No. 9 in D minor	MMO CD 3306
J.S. BACH Flute Sonata No. 1 in B minor, BWV1030/KUHLAU Two Duets (2 CD set)	MMO CD 3344
J.S. BACH Suite No. 2 for Flute & Strings in B minor, BWV1067	MMO CD 3302
J.S. BACH 'Triple' Concerto in A minor, BWV1044; VIVALDI Concerto in D minor	MMO CD 3307
Band Aids: Concert Band Favorites with Orchestra	MMO CD 3352
Beginning Contest Solos, vol. I	MMO CD 3321
Beginning Contest Solos, vol. II	MMO CD 3322
Beginning Contest Solos, vol. III	MMO CD 3330
BOCCHERINI Flute Concerto in D major; VIVALDI Flute Concerto No. 2 in G minor 'La Notte'; MOZART Andante for Flute and Strings	MMO CD 3303
BOLLING Suite for Flute and Jazz Piano Trio	MMO CD 3342
Classic Themes: Student Editions, 27 Easy Songs (2nd-3rd year)	MMO CD 3355
Concert Band Favorites with Orchestra	MMO CD 3351
Easy Flute Solos: Beginning Students, vol. I	MMO CD 3316
Easy Flute Solos: Beginning Students, vol. II (New Digitally Remastered Version) (2CD Set)	MMO CD 3317
Easy Jazz Duets for Two Flutes and Rhythm Section	MMO CD 3318
First Chair Solos with Orchestral Accompaniment	MMO CD 3333
Flute & Guitar Duets, vol. I	MMO CD 3319
Flute & Guitar Duets, vol. II (2CD Set)	MMO CD 3320
Flute Song: Easy Familiar Classics with Orchestra	MMO CD 3313
HANDEL / MARCELLO / TELEMANN Sonatas in F major	MMO CD 3350
HANDEL Three Sonatas for Flute & Piano; TELEMANN Three Duet Sonatas for Two Flutes (2 CD Set)	MMO CD 3343
HAYDN Divertimento in D major; VIVALDI Concerto in D major, op. 10 No. 3 'Bullfinch'; FREDERICK THE GREAT Concerto in C major	MMO CD 3304
HAYDN Four 'London' Trios for 2 Flutes & Violoncello, HobIV:1-4	MMO CD 3309

All MMO albums shown here, may be viewed for their contents at: www.musicminusone.com

HAYDN Three Trios: F major (HobXV:17),
D major (HobXV:16), and G major(HobXV:15) ....MMO CD 3363
Intermediate Contest Solos, vol. I ....MMO CD 3323
Intermediate Contest Solos, vol. II ....MMO CD 3324
Intermediate Contest Solos, vol. III ....MMO CD 3327
Intermediate Contest Solos, vol. IV ....MMO CD 3331
Jewels for Woodwind Quintet ....MMO CD 3336
The Joy of Woodwind Music...MMO CD 3335
KUHLAU Trio in E-flat major / BACH Flute Sonatas
in E-flat and A major (2 CD set) ....MMO CD 3345
MOZART Concerto for Flute & Harp in
C major, KV299 (2 CD Set) ....MMO CD 3361
MOZART Flute Concerto in G major, KV313 ....MMO CD 3301
MOZART Flute Concerto No. 2 in D major, KV314;
QUANTZ Flute Concerto in G major)...MMO CD 3362
MOZART Quartet in F major, KV370;
STAMITZ Quartet in F major, op. 8, no. 3 ....MMO CD 3308
MOZART Three Flute Quartets in D major, A major and C major ....MMO CD 3311
PEPUSCH Sonata in C / TELEMANN Sonata in C minor......................MMO CD 3346
PIAZZOLA Histoire du Tango and other Latin Classics
for Flute & Guitar Duet..MMO CD 3364
QUANTZ Trio Sonata in C minor; BACH Gigue;
ABEL Sonata No. 2 in F major..MMO CD 3347
Teacher's Partner: Basic Flute Studies, first year ....MMO CD 3334
TELEMANN Concerto No. 1 in D major/
CORRETTE Sonata in E minor...MMO CD 3348
TELEMANN Suite A minor; GLUCK 'Orpheus' scene;
PERGOLESI Concerto G major (2CD Set)....................................MMO CD 3312
TELEMANN Trio in F major / B-flat major
HANDEL Sonata No. 3 in C major ....MMO CD 3349
Three Sonatas for Alto Recorder, Harpsichord & Viola da gamba
(Handel, Telemann, & Marcello)..MMO CD 3340
VERACINI Four Sonatas for Flute, Alto/Treble Recorder
or Violin with Harpsicohrd ....MMO CD 3370
VIVALDI Flute Concerti in D major (RV427);
F major (RV434); G major (RV438)...MMO CD 3314
VIVALDI Flute Concerti in D major (RV429);
G major (RV435); A minor (RV440) ....MMO CD 3315
VIVALDI Flute Concerto in F major; TELEMANN Flute Concerto in D major;
LECLAIR Flute Concerto in C major ....MMO CD 3305
World Favorites: Student Editions, 41 Easy Selections (1st-2nd year) ....MMO CD 3354

French Horn

Advanced Contest Solos, vol. I ....MMO CD 3515
Advanced Contest Solos, vol. II ....MMO CD 3516
Advanced Contest Solos, vol. III ....MMO CD 3518
Band Aids: Concert Band Favorites with Orchestra ....MMO CD 3524
Baroque Brass and Beyond: Brass Quintets...................................MMO CD 3502
BEETHOVEN Quintet for Piano and Winds in E-flat major, op. 16 ....MMO CD 3505
Beginning Contest Solos, vol. I ....MMO CD 3511
Beginning Contest Solos, vol. II ....MMO CD 3512
French Horn Up Front Brass Quintets ....MMO CD 3522
French Horn Woodwind Music...MMO CD 3520
Horn of Plenty Brass Quintets ....MMO CD 3523
Intermediate Contest Solos, vol. I ....MMO CD 3513
Intermediate Contest Solos, vol. II ....MMO CD 3514
Intermediate Contest Solos, vol. III ....MMO CD 3517
Intermediate Contest Solos, vol. IV ....MMO CD 3519
Masterpieces for Woodwind Quintet ....MMO CD 3521
MOZART Horn Concerto No. 2 in E-flat major, KV417;
Horn Conerto No. 3 in E-flat major, KV447 ....MMO CD 3501
MOZART Quintet for Piano and Winds in E-flat major, KV452.............MMO CD 3506
MOZART Twelve Pieces for Two Horns, KV487 ....MMO CD 3504
Music for Brass Ensemble..MMO CD 3503

Visit our two websites: www.musicminusone.com and www.pocketsongs.com

Guitar

Bluegrass Guitar..................................MMO CD 3608
BOCCHERINI Guitar Quintet No. 4
in D 'Fandango' ....MMO CD 3601
Classic Guitar Duets ....MMO CD 3603
Classical & Romantic Guitar Duets ....MMO CD 3605
Cool Jazz for Guitar ....MMO CD 3620
Favorite Folks Songs For Guitar ....MMO CD 3611
For Guitarists Only! Jimmy Raney
Small Band Arrangements ....MMO CD 3612
GIULIANI Guitar Concerto No. 1
in A major, op. 30 ....MMO CD 3617
GIULIANI Guitar Quintet in A major, op. 65..MMO CD 3602
Guitar and Flute Duets, vol. I (2CD Set) ....MMO CD 3606
Guitar and Flute Duets, vol. II (2CD Set) ......MMO CD 3607
How To Play the Folk Guitar (2 CD Set) ....MMO CD 3610
Orchestral Gems for Classical Guitar ....MMO CD 3615
PIAZZOLA Histoire du Tango and other Latin Classics
for Guitar & Flute Duet ....MMO CD 3619
Play The Blues Guitar:
A Dick Weissman Method ....MMO CD 3614
Play the Guitar: The Easy Way to Learn the Chords and
Rhythms, by George Barnes & Bob Mersey ..MMO CD 3609
Renaissance & Baroque Guitar Duets ....MMO CD 3604
RODRIGO Concierto de Aranjuez.................MMO CD 3616
Ten Duets for Two Guitars ....MMO CD 3613

Harp

MOZART Concerto for Flute & Harp in C major,
KV299 (2CD Set) ....MMO CD 5201

Instructional - Music & Musicians

Art Of Improvisation, Vol. I ....MMOCD 7005
Art Of Improvisation, Vol. II ....MMOCD 7006
The Blues Minus You ....MMO CD 7007
Evolution of the Blues ....MMO CD 7004
Jazz Improvisation: a complete course
(5 CDs)..MMO CD 7012
Rutgers University Music Dictation
and Ear Training (7 CD Set) ....MMO CD 7001
Take a Chorus minus B-flat/E-flat
Instruments ....MMO CD 7008
Twelve Classic Jazz Standards:
B-flat/E-flat/Bass Clef ....MMO CD 7010
Twelve More Classic Jazz Standards:
B-flat/E-flat/Bass Clef ....MMO CD 7011
Understanding Jazz ....MMO CD 7009

Oboe

ALBINONI Oboe Concerti B-flat, op. 7 no. 3; D major,
op. 7, no. 6; D minor, op. 9, no. 2 ....MMO CD 3400
J.S. BACH Brandenburg Concerto No. 2;
TELEMANN Concerto in A minor....................MMO CD 3403
BEETHOVEN Quintet for Piano and
Winds in E-flat major, op. 16 ....MMO CD 3409
The Joy of Woodwind Quintets ....MMO CD 3406
Masterpieces for Woodwind Quintet ....MMO CD 3405
MOZART Quartet in F major, KV370;
STAMITZ Quartet in F major, op. 8, no. 3......MMO CD 3402
Oboe Classics For Beginner...........................MMO CD 3411
Oboe Classics For The Advanced Player ....MMO CD 3413
Oboe Classics For The Intermediate Player ..MMO CD 3412
Oboe Concerti: TELEMANN F minor;
 HANDEL B-flat major; VIVALDI D minor ......MMO CD 3401
The Oboe Soloist: Classic Solos
for Oboe (2 CD Set)..MMO CD 3404
PEPUSCH Trio Sonata in C major;
TELEMANN Trio Sonata in C minor ....MMO CD 3407
QUANTZ Trio Sonata in C minor;
BACH Gigue (from Trio Sonata No. 1 in C major);
BACH Trio Sonata in G minor ....MMO CD 3408

Piano

2+2=5: A Study in Odd Times ....MMO CD 2045
ARENSKY 6 Pièces Enfantines, op. 34; STRAVINSKY 3 Easy
Pieces (Dances) (2nd-3rd year) ....MMO CD 3028
ARENSKY Concerto for Piano
in F major, op. 2...MMO CD 3080
The Art Of Popular Piano Playing, vol. I
Student Level ....MMO CD 3033
The Art Of Popular Piano Playing, vol. II
Student Level (2 CD Set) ....MMO CD 3034
C.P.E. BACH Piano Concerto in A minor,
Wq26, H430...MMO CD 3059
C.P.E. BACH Piano Concerto
in D minor, Wq23 ....MMO CD 3091
J.S. BACH Brandenburg Concerto
No. 5 in D major, BWV1050 ....MMO CD 3054
J.S. BACH Concerto for 2 Pianos C minor, BWV1060;
SCHUMANN Andante & Variations for 2 Pianos,
Violoncelli & Horn ....MMO CD 3055
J.S. BACH Keyboard Concerto
in D minor, BWV1052 ....MMO CD 3022
J.S. BACH Keyboard Concerto in F minor, BWV1056;
J.C. BACH Piano Concerto in E-flat major ......MMO CD 3021
J.S. BACH 'Triple' Concerto in A minor, BWV1044;
Brandenburg Concerto No. 5
in D major (1st mvmt) ....MMO CD 3057

Piano - continued

BEETHOVEN Piano Concerto No. 1 in C major, op. 15 ....MMO CD 3001
BEETHOVEN Piano Concerto No. 2 in B-flat major, op. 19 ....MMO CD 3002
BEETHOVEN Piano Concerto No. 3 in C minor, op. 37 ....MMO CD 6003
BEETHOVEN Piano Concerto No. 4 in G major, op. 58 ....MMO CD 3004
BEETHOVEN Piano Concerto No. 5 in E-flat major, op. 73 ....MMO CD 6005
BEETHOVEN Piano Trio No. 8 in E-flat major, WoO38 & Trio No. 11
in G major ('Kakadu' Variations), op. 121a ....MMO CD 3065
BEETHOVEN Quintet for Piano and Winds in E-flat major, op. 16 ....MMO CD 3070
BEETHOVEN Three Marches (4th-5th year) ....MMO CD 3032
BIZET Jeux d'enfants (Twelve Children's Games), op. 22 ....MMO CD 3043
Blues Fusion for Piano ....MMO CD 3049
BOLLING Suite for Flute and Jazz Piano Trio ....MMO CD 3050
BRAHMS Piano Concerto No. 1 in D minor (2 CD Set) ....MMO CD 3009
CHOPIN Piano Concerto in E minor, op. 11 (2 CD Set) ....MMO CD 3010
CHOPIN Piano Concerto in F minor, op. 21 ....MMO CD 3075
DEBUSSY Petite Suite (Four Pieces for piano duet) ....MMO CD 3030
DIABELLI Pleasures of Youth, op. 163 ....MMO CD 3046
DVORAK Piano Trio in A major, op. 90 'Dumky' ....MMO CD 3037
DVORAK Quintet in A major, op. 81 ....MMO CD 3038
FAURE 'Dolly' Suite, op. 56 (six pieces for piano duet) ....MMO CD 3029
From Dixie to Swing ....MMO CD 3053
GERSHWIN Rhapsody in Blue ....MMO CD 3083
GLAZUNOV Piano Concerto No. 1 in F minor, op. 92 ....MMO CD 3078
GRETCHANINOV On the Green Meadow ....MMO CD 3044
GRIEG Piano Concerto in A minor, op.16 ....MMO CD 3006
HANDEL Concerto Grosso in D major, op. 3, no. 6; HAYDN Concertino in C major;
J.C. BACH Piano Concerto in B-flat major, op.13, no. 4 ....MMO CD 3056
HAYDN Piano Concerto in D major, HobXVIII/11 ....MMO CD 3023
HAYDN Piano Trios, vol. II: G major (HobXV:25), F-sharp minor
(HobXV:26), and F major (HobXV:6) ....MMO CD 3076
The Heart of the Piano Concerto ....MMO CD 3024
The Jim Odrich Experience, with Orchestra: Pop Piano Played Easy ....MMO CD 3062
LISZT Piano Concerto No. 1 in E-flat major, S124; WEBER Konzertstück, op. 79 ..MMO CD 3019
LISZT Piano Concerto No. 2 in A major, S125; Hungarian Fantasia, S123 ....MMO CD 3020
MACDOWELL Piano Concerto No. 2 in D minor, op. 23 ....MMO CD 3090
MAYKAPAR First Steps, op. 29 ....MMO CD 3041
MENDELSSOHN Capriccio Brilliant; FRANCK Variations Symphoniques (Symphonic Variations)
for Piano & Orchestra, M46 ....MMO CD 3058
MENDELSSOHN Piano Concerto No. 1 in G minor, op. 25 ....MMO CD 3011
MENDELSSOHN Piano Trio No. 1 in D major, op. 49 ....MMO CD 3039
MENDELSSOHN Piano Trio No. 2 in C minor, op. 66 ....MMO CD 3040
MOZART Complete Music for Piano 4 Hands (2 CD Set) ....MMO CD 3036
MOZART Piano Concerto No. 9 in E-flat major, KV271 ....MMO CD 3012
MOZART Piano Concerto No. 12 in A major, KV414 ....MMO CD 30138
MOZART Piano Concerto No. 14 in E-flat major, KV449 ....MMO CD 3073
MOZART Piano Concerto No. 17 in G major, KV453 ....MMO CD 30188
MOZART Piano Concerto No. 19 in F major, KV459 ....MMO CD 3081
MOZART Piano Concerto No. 20 in D minor, KV466 ....MMO CD 3014
MOZART Piano Concerto No. 21 in C major, KV467 'Elvira Madigan' ..MMO CD 3072
MOZART Piano Concerto No. 23 in A major, KV488 ....MMO CD 3015
MOZART Piano Concerto No. 23 in A major, KV488 ....MMO CD 3098
MOZART Piano Concerto No. 24 in C minor, KV491 ....MMO CD 3016
MOZART Piano Concerto No. 25 in C major, KV503 'Olympian' or 'Emperor' ....MMO CD 3092
MOZART Piano Concerto No. 26 in D major, KV537, 'Coronation' (2CD set) ......MMO CD 3017
MOZART Piano Concerto No. 27 in B-flat major, KV595 ....MMO CD 3082
MOZART Quintet for Piano and Winds in E-flat major, KV452 ....MMO CD 3071
Opera Arias for Piano & Orchestra: Jim Odrich arrangements ....MMO CD 3048
'Pop' Piano For Starters (Student Level) ....MMO CD 3035
Popular Piano Made Easy, with Orchestra: Arranged by Jim Odrich ..MMO CD 3063
POZZOLI Smiles of Childhood ....MMO CD 3045
RACHMANINOV Piano Concerto No. 2 in C minor, op. 18 ....MMO CD 3007
RACHMANINOV Piano Concerto No. 3 in D minor, op.30 (2CD set) ....MMO CD 3074
RACHMANINOV Six Scenes ....MMO CD 3027
RAVEL Piano Trio in A minor ....MMO CD 3061

RIMSKY-KORSAKOV Piano Concerto in C-sharp minor, op. 30; ARENSKY Fantasia on Russian Folksongs, op. 48 ....MMO CD 3086

RUBINSTEIN Piano Concerto No. 4 in D minor, op. 70 ....MMO CD 3079

SCHUBERT Fantasie in F minor, op. 103, D940; Grand Sonata in B-flat major, op. 30, D617 ..MMO CD 3047

SCHUBERT Piano Quintet in A major, op. 114, D667 'Forellen-Quintett' or 'Trout Quintet' ....MMO CD 3087

SCHUBERT Piano Trio in B-flat major, op. 99 (2 CD Set) ....MMO CD 3066

SCHUBERT Piano Trio in E-flat major, op. 100 (2 CD Set) ....MMO CD 3067

SCHUMANN Piano Concerto in A minor, op. 54 ....MMO CD 3008

SCHUMANN Piano Trio in D minor, op. 63 ..MMO CD 3064

SCHUMANN Six Impromptus ('Bilder aus Osten'/ 'Pictures from the East'), op. 66; Children's Ball, op. 130 ....MMO CD 3031

Sinatra Standards for Piano and Orchestra: Arranged by Jim Odrich..........................MMO CD 3069

STRETCHIN' OUT: 'Comping' with a Jazz Rhythm Section ....MMO CD 3060

TCHAIKOVSKY Fifty Russian Folk Songs ....MMO CD 3042

TCHAIKOVSKY Piano Concerto No. 1 in B-flat minor, op. 23 ....MMO CD 3026

Themes from Great Piano Concerti...............MMO CD 3025

Twenty Dixieland Classics ....MMO CD 3051

Twenty Rhythm Backgrounds to Standards ....MMO CD 3052

Recorder (alto or soprano)

Echoes of Time (2 CD SET) ....MMO CD 3357

Recorder (alto)

Eighteenth Century Recorder Music (2 CD SET) ....MMO CD 3358

Three Sonatas for Alto Recorder, Harpsichord & Viola da gamba (Telemann & Handel)............MMO CD 3341

You Can Play The Recorder: Beginning Adult Method ....MMO CD 3339

Recorder (soprano)

English Consort Music (2 CD SET)................MMO CD 3359

Let's Play The Recorder: Beginning Children's Method ....MMO CD 3338

Playing The Recorder: Folk Songs of Many Nations ....MMO CD 3337

Renaissance Dances and Fantasias ....MMO CD 3356

Recorder (soprano, alto, tenor, or bass)

Dances of Three Centuries ....MMOCD 3360

Soprano Saxophone

Music for Saxophone Quartet ....MMO CD 4801

Stompin' & Struttin' the New Swing: Six Bands on a Hot Tin Roof ....,.....MMO CD 4802

Tenor Saxophone

Band Aids: Concert Band Favorites with Orchestra ....MMO CD 4213

Bluesaxe: Blues for Saxophone, trumpet or clarinet..............................MMO CD 4205

Cool Jazz (Rich Maraday)............................MMO CD 4216

Days of Wine & Roses: Sax Section Minus You ....MMO CD 4210

Easy Jazz Duets for Two Tenor Saxophones and Rhythm Section..............................MMO CD 4203

Easy Tenor Saxophone Solos: Student Edition, volume 1 ....MMO CD 4201

Easy Tenor Saxophone Solos: Student Edition, volume 2 ....MMO CD 4202

For Saxes Only: Arranged by Bob Wilber, for alto, tenor, baritone sax, trumpet or clarinet...................MMO CD 4204

JOBIM Brazilian Bossa Novas with Strings ....MMO CD 4206

Music for Saxophone Quartet ....MMO CD 4211

Play Lead in a Sax Section ....MMO CD 4209

Popular Concert Favorites with Orchestra ....MMO CD 4212

Sinatra, Sax and Swing (Brian Hayes) ....MMO CD 4217

Stompin' & Struttin' the New Swing: Six Bands on a Hot Tin Roof ....MMO CD 4215

Tenor Jazz Jam (2 CD Set) ....MMO CD 4214

Twenty Dixieland Classics ....MMO CD 4207

Twenty Rhythm Backgrounds to Standards ....MMO CD 4208

Trombone

Advanced Contest Solos, vol. I ....MMO CD 3915

Advanced Contest Solos, vol. II ....MMO CD 3916

Advanced Contest Solos, vol. III ....MMO CD 3917

Advanced Contest Solos, vol. III ....MMO CD 3918

Advanced Contest Solos, vol. V ....MMO CD 3919

Band Aids: Concert Band Favorites ....MMO CD 3930

Baroque Brass and Beyond: Brass Quintets ..MMO CD 3904

Beginning Contest Solos, vol. I ....MMO CD 3911

Beginning Contest Solos, vol. II...................MMO CD 3912

Big Band Ballads for Tenor or Bass Trombone ....MMO CD 3907

Classic Themes: Student Editions, 27 Easy Songs (2nd-3rd year) ....MMO CD 3932

Classical Trombone Solos (2 CD Set) ....MMO CD 3909

Easy Jazz Duets for Two Trombones and Rhythm Section..............................MMO CD 3903

Easy Trombone Solos: Student Level, vol, I....MMO CD 3901

Easy Trombone Solos: Student Level, vol, II ..MMO CD 3902

For Trombones Only: More Brass Quintets ..MMO CD 3928

From Dixie to Swing....................................MMO CD 3926

Intermediate Contest Solos, vol. I ....MMO CD 3913

Intermediate Contest Solos, vol. II ....MMO CD 3914

Jazz Standards with Strings (2 CD Set) ....MMO CD 3910

Music for Brass Ensemble ....MMO CD 3905

Popular Concert Favorites with Orchestra ....MMO CD 3929

Sticks & Bones Brass Quintets......................MMO CD 3927

STRAVINSKY L'Histoire du Soldat (septet)......MMO CD 3908

Teacher's Partner: Basic Studies, first year ....MMO CD 3920

Twenty Dixieland Classics ....MMO CD 3924

Twenty Rhythm Backgrounds to Standards ....MMO CD 3925

Unsung Hero: Great Sinatra Standards ....MMO CD 3906

World Favorites: Student Editions, 41 Easy Selections (1st-2nd year)..............................MMO CD 3931

All MMO albums shown here, may be viewed for their specific contents at: www.musicminusone.com

Trumpet

2+2=5: A Study in Odd Times ....MMO CD 2043
Advanced Contest Solos, vol. I ....MMO CD 3815
Advanced Contest Solos, vol. II ....MMO CD 3818
Advanced Contest Solos, vol. III ....MMO CD 3819
Art of the Solo Trumpet with Orchestral Accompaniment ....MMO CD 3807
Band Aids: Concert Band Favorites with Orchestra ....MMO CD 3832
Baroque Brass and Beyond: Brass Quintets ....MMO CD 3808
Beginning Contest Solos, vol. I ....MMO CD 3811
Beginning Contest Solos, vol. II ....MMO CD 3812
Beginning Contest Solos, vol. III ....MMO CD 3820
Beginning Contest Solos, vol. IV ....MMO CD 3821
Brass Trax: The Trumpet Artistry Of David O'Neill ....MMO CD 3833
Classic Pieces for Trumpet & Organ (2CD Set) ....MMO CD 3840
Classic Themes: Student Editions, 27 Easy Songs (2nd-3rd year)......MMO CD 3837
Classic Trumpet Solos with Piano Accompaniment ....MMO CD 3830
Complete Arban Duets: all of the classic studies ....MMO CD 3809
Contest Solos (Armando Ghitalla) ....MMO CD 3816
Easy Jazz Duets for Two Trumpets and Rhythm Section ....MMO CD 3804
First Chair Trumpet Solos with Orchestral Accompaniment ....MMO CD 3806
From Dixie to Swing...MMO CD 3826
HAYDN Concerto in E-flat major, HobVIIe:1; TELEMANN Trumpet Concerto in D;
FASCH Trumpet Concerto in D ....MMO CD 3801
Intermediate Contest Solos, vol. I ....MMO CD 3813
Intermediate Contest Solos, vol. II ....MMO CD 3814
Intermediate Contest Solos, vol. III ....MMO CD 3817
Intermediate Contest Solos, vol. IV ....MMO CD 3822
Modern Brass Quintets ....MMO CD 3828
Music for Brass Ensemble ....MMO CD 3805
Popular Concert Favorites for Trumpet with Orchestra ....MMO CD 3831
SOUSA Marches plus BEETHOVEN, BERLIOZ, STRAUSS ....MMO CD 3810
Stompin' & Struttin' the New Swing: Six Bands on a Hot Tin Roof ....MMO CD 3838
STRAVINSKY L'Histoire du Soldat (septet)....................................MMO CD 3835
Teacher's Partner: Basic Trumpet Studies, first year....................MMO CD 3823
Trumpet Pieces: Brass Quintets..MMO CD 3827
Trumpet Solos: Student Level, vol. I ....MMO CD 3802
Trumpet Solos: Student Level, vol. II..MMO CD 3803
Trumpet Triumphant: The Further Adventures Of David O'Neill ....MMO CD 3834
Twenty Dixieland Classics ....MMO CD 3824
Twenty Rhythm Backgrounds to Standards ....MMO CD 3825
When Jazz Was Young: The Bob Wilber All Stars ....MMO CD 3829
World Favorites: Student Editions, 41 Easy Selections (1st-2nd year) ....MMO CD 3836

Tuba/Bass Trombone

He's Not Heavy, He's My Tuba ....MMO CD 4701
Music for Brass Ensemble ....MMO CD 4703
Sweets for Brass...MMO CD 4702

Vibes

For Vibists Only!: The Shelly Elias Vibraphone Method, vol. I ....MMO CD 5101
Good Vibe-rations: The Shelly Elias Vibraphone Method, vol. II ....MMO CD 5102

Viola

BEETHOVEN String Quartet in A minor, op. 132 (2 CD Set) ....MMO CD 4503
DVORAK Quintet in A major, op. 81 ....MMO CD 4504
DVORAK String Trio 'Terzetto' in C major, op. 74, B148 (2 Violins/Viola) ......MMO CD 4502
HOFFMEISTER Concerto for Viola and Orchestra in D major ....MMO CD 4505
SCHUBERT Piano Quintet in A major, op. 114, D667 'Trout Quintet' ....MMO CD 4506
Viola Solos with piano accompaniment ....MMO CD 4501

Violin

18th Century Violin Pieces for Violin & Orchestra ......MMO CD 3121

Air on a G String: Favorite Encores
with Orchestra (Easy-Medium) ....MMO CD 3119

J.S. BACH Brandenburg Concerti Nos. 4 in G major
(BWV1048) & 5 in D major (BWV1050) ....MMO CD 3105

J.S. BACH Brandenburg Concerto No. 2;
'Triple' Concerto in A minor, BWV1044 ....MMO CD 3106

J.S. BACH 'Double' Concerto in D minor, BWV1043 ..MMO CD 3103

J.S. BACH Violin Concerto in D minor (from Concerto
No. 1 for Harpsichord, BWV1052)........MMO CD 3107

J.S. BACH Violin Concerto No. 1 in A minor, BWV1041;
Violin Concerto in E major, BWV1042........MMO CD 3104

Beautiful Music for Two Violins, vol. I: 1st position ....MMO CD 3137

Beautiful Music for Two Violins, vol. II: 2nd position ..MMO CD 3138

Beautiful Music for Two Violins, vol. III: 3rd position..MMO CD 3139

Beautiful Music for Two Violins, vol. IV:
1st, 2nd, 3rd position ....MMO CD 3140

BEETHOVEN Piano Trio No. 8 in E-flat major, WoO 38,
& No. 11 in G major, 'Kakadu,' op. 121a ....MMO CD 3153

BEETHOVEN String Quartet in A minor,
op. 132 (2 CD Set) ....MMO CD 3156

BEETHOVEN String Quartets No. 1 in F major
& No. 4 in C minor, op. 18 ....MMO CD 3158

BEETHOVEN Two Romances for Violin & Orchestra;
Sonata No. 5 in F major 'Spring' ....MMO CD 3115

BEETHOVEN Violin Concertoin D op. 61 (2 CD Set)......MMO D 3117

BRAHMS Double Concerto for Violin &
Violoncello in A minor, op. 102 (2CD set)........MMO CD 3171

BRAHMS Violin Concerto in D major, op. 77 ....MMO CD 3108

BRUCH Violin Concerto No. 1 in G minor, op. 26 ......MMO CD 3100

BRUCH Violin Concerto No. 2 in D minor, op. 44 ......MMO CD 3172

CHAUSSON Poeme for violin and orchestra, op. 25;
SCHUBERT Rondo in A major, D438........MMO CD 3109

Concert Pieces for the Serious Violinist
(Easy-Medium) ....MMOCD 3120

Concertmaster The: Solos from
Symphonic Works (with Orchestral) ....MMO CD 3118

DVORAK Quintet in A major, op. 81 ....MMO CD 3157

DVORAK String Trio 'Terzetto' in C major,
op. 74, B148 (2 violins & viola) ....MMO CD 3143

GLAZUNOV Violin Concerto in A minor, op. 82 ....MMO CD 3168

Great Scott: Joplin's Ragtime String Quartets:
The Zinn String Quartet........MMO CD 3151

HAYDN Piano Trios, vol. I: F major (HobXV:17), D major
(HobXV:16), and G major(HobXV:15) ....MMO CD 3159

HAYDN String Quartet in B-flat major,
'Sunrise,' op. 76, no. 4, HobIII:78 ....MMO CD 3134

HAYDN String Quartet in C major,
'Emperor,' op. 76, no. 3, HobIII:77 ....MMO CD 3133

HAYDN String Quartet in D major,
'Largo,' op. 76, no. 5, HobIII:79 ....MMO CD 3135

HAYDN String Quartet in D minor, 'Fifths'/'The Bell'/'The
Donkey,' op. 76, no. 2, HobIII:76 ....MMO CD 3132

HAYDN String Quartet in E-flat major,
op. 76, no. 6, HobIII:80 ....MMO CD 3136

HAYDN String Quartet in G major,
'Erdödy,' op. 76, no. 1, HobIII:75 ....MMO CD 3131

The Heart of the Violin Concerto ....MMO CD 3141

Jascha Heifitz Favorite Encores (2 CD Set) ....MMO CD 3164

KORNGOLD Violin Concerto in D major, op. 35 ....MMO CD 3166

KREISLER Favorite Encores (2 CD Set) ....MMO CD 3165

LALO Symphonie Espagnole, op. 21 ....MMO CD 3110

MENDELSSOHN Violin Concerto in E minor, op. 64....MMO CD 3101

Mischa Elman Concert Favorites (2 CD Set) ....MMO CD 3163

Mischa Elman Favorite Encores (2 CD Set) ....MMO CD 3162

MOZART Violin Concerto No. 1 in B-flat major, KV207;
Rondo Concertant in B-flat major, KV269 ......MMO CD 3161
MOZART Violin Concerto No. 3
in G major, KV216 ......MMO CD 3160
MOZART Violin Concerto No. 4 in D major, KV218;
VIVALDI Concerto in A minor, op.3 no.6........MMO CD 3111
MOZART Violin Concerto No. 5
in A major, KV219 ......MMO CD 3112
Orchestral Favorites, vol. I (Easy Level)..........MMO CD 3122
Orchestral Favorites, vol. II (Med. Level) ......MMO CD 3123
Orchestral Favorites, volume III
(Medium-Difficult Level) ......MMO CD 3124
PROKOFIEV Violin Concerto No. 1 in D major,
op. 19 (1915-1917) ......MMO CD 3178
RAVEL Piano Trio in A minor ......MMO CD 3147
SAINT-SAENS Introduction & Rondo Capriccioso
for Violin & Orchestra; MOZART Serenade No. 5, K204;
Adagio, KV261 ......MMO CD 3116
SCHUBERT Piano Quintet in A major, op. 114, D667
'Forellen-Quintett' or 'Trout Quintet' ......MMO CD 3169
SCHUBERT Piano Trio in B-flat major,
op. 99 (2 CD Set) ......MMO CD 3154
SCHUBERT Piano Trio in E-flat major,
op. 100 (2 CD Set) ......MMO CD 3155
SCHUBERT Three Sonatinas
(Robert Zubrycki, soloist) ......MMO CD 3130
SCHUMANN Piano Trio in D minor, op. 63 ..MMO CD 3152
SIBELIUS Violin Concerto in D minor, op. 47 MMO CD 3144
STRAVINSKY L'Histoire du Soldat (septet)......MMO CD 3146
TCHAIKOVSKY Violin Concerto
in D major, op. 35 ......MMO CD 3102
Teacher's Partner: Basic Violin Studies,
first year ......MMO CD 3142
Themes from the major Violin Concerti ......MMO CD 3145
The Three Bs: Bach/Beethoven/Brahms
for Violin & Orchestra ......MMO CD 3125
VIOTTI Violin Concerto No. 22 in A minor ....MMO CD 3114
VIVALDI 'Le Quattre Stagioni' ('The Four Seasons')
for violin and orchestra, op. 8,
nos. 1-4 (2 CD Set) ......MMO CD 3127
VIVALDI 'L'Estro Armonico': Violin Concerti in A minor,
op. 3, no. 6, RV356; Concerto Grosso in A minor,
op. 3, no. 8, RV522; Concerto in D major
op. 3, no.9, RV230 ......MMO CD 3126
VIVALDI Violin Concerto in E major, op. 3, no. 12, RV265;
Violin Concerto in C major, op. 8,
no.6, RV180 'Il Piacere' ......MMO CD 3129
VIVALDI Violin Concerto in E-flat major, 'La Tempesta di
Mare' op. 8, no. 5, RV236; ALBINONI Violin
Concerto in A major......MMO CD 3128
WIENIAWSKI Violin Concerto No. 2 in D minor, op. 22;
SARASATE Zigeunerweisen ('Gypsy Ways'),
op. 20......MMO CD 3113

Violoncello

C.P.E. BACH Violoncello Concerto
in A minor, Wq170/H432................................MMO CD 3702
BEETHOVEN Piano Trio No. 8 in E-flat major, WoO38
& Trio No. 11 in G major ('Kakadu' Variations),
op. 121a ......MMO CD 3710
BEETHOVEN String Quartet in A minor,
op. 132 (2 CD Set) ......MMO CD 3713
BEETHOVEN Violoncello Sonata in A major, op. 69;
TELEMANN Violoncello Duet in B-flat............MMO CD 3715
BOCCHERINI Violoncello Concerto in B-flat;
BRUCH Kol Nidrei ......MMO CD 3703

BOLLING Suite For Violoncello
and Jazz Piano Trio ......MMO CD 3706
BRAHMS Double Concerto for Violoncello
& Violin in A minor, op. 102 ......MMO CD 3722
DVORAK Quintet in A major, op. 81 ......MMO CD 3714
DVORAK Violoncello Concerto in B minor,
op. 104 (2 CD Set) ......MMO CD 3701
ELGAR Violoncello Concerto
in E minor, op. 85 ......MMO CD 3720
Great Scott! Ragtime Minus You ......MMO CD 3708
HAYDN Piano Trios, vol. II: G major (HobXV:25),
F-sharp minor (HobXV:26), and F major
(HobXV:6) minus Violoncello ......MMO CD 3717
HAYDN Violoncello Concerto
in C major, HobVIIb:1 ......MMO CD 3718
HAYDN Violoncello Concerto
in D major, HobVIIb:2 ......MMO CD 3719
RAVEL Piano Trio in A minor ......MMO CD 3707
SCHUBERT Piano Quintet in A major, op. 114, D667
'Forellen-Quintett' or 'Trout Quintet' ......MMO CD 3721
SCHUBERT Piano Trio in B-flat major,
op. 99 (2 CD Set) ......MMO CD 3711
SCHUBERT Piano Trio in E-flat major,
op. 100 (2 CD Set) ......MMO CD 3712
SCHUMANN Concerto for Violoncello and Orchestra
in A minor, op. 129; Romantic Concertpieces for 'Cello
and Piano ......MMO CD 3705
SCHUMANN Piano Trio
in D minor, op. 63 ......MMO CD 3709
Ten Concert Pieces for Violoncello
and Piano ......MMO CD 3704
The Cello Soloist: Classic Solos for Cello
and Piano ......MMO CD 3726
WINER Violoncello Concerto; SCHUBERT Ave Maria;
SAINT-SAENS Allegro Appassionato ......MMO CD 3716

Vocal

LEHAR Highlights from Die Lustige Witwe
(The Merry Widow) ......MMO CD 4074
Ten More Classic Vocal Standards ......MMO CD 4051
Twelve Classic Vocal Standards ......MMO CD 4050

Vocal Alto

Oratorio Arias For Alto ......MMO CD 4031

Vocal Bass-Baritone

17th/18th Century Italian Songs - Low Voice,
Volume 1 ....MMO CD 4012
17th/18th Century Italian Songs - Low Voice,
Volume 2 ....MMO CD 4014
Bass-Baritone Arias with Orchestra, vol. I ..MMO CDG 4056
Bass-Baritone Arias with Orchestra, vol. II..MMO CDG 4066
BRAHMS German Lieder - Low Voice ....MMO CD 4006
Everybody's Favorite Songs - Low Voice,
Volume 1 ....MMO CDG 4008
Everybody's Favorite Songs - Low Voice,
Volume 2 ....MMO CDG 4010
Famous Baritone Arias ....MMO CDG 4018
Famous Bass Arias....................MMO CDG 4019
Italian Opera Arias for Bass-Baritone
and Orchestra ....MMO CDG 4071
Oratorio Arias For Bass ....MMO CD 4033
SCHUBERT German Lieder - Low Voice,
Volume 2 ....MMO CDG 4004
SCHUMANN German Lieder For Low Voice ..MMO CD 4025
STRAUSS German Lieder For Low Voice ....MMO CD 4023
VERDI Bass-Baritone Arias with Orchestra ....MMO CD 4078
WOLF German Lieder For Low Voice ....MMO CD 4021

Vocal Contralto

Beginning Contralto Solos.........................MMO CD 4046

Vocal Mezzo-Soprano

Famous Mezzo-Soprano Arias.....................MMO CDG 4016
French & Italian Opera Arias for Mezzo-Soprano
and Orchestra ....MMO CDG 4062
French Mezzo-Soprano Arias
with Orchestra ....MMO CDG 4086
VERDI Arias for Mezzo-Soprano
with Orchestra ....MMO CDG 4055

Vocal Soprano

17th/18th Century Italian Songs
High Voice, Volume 1 ....MMO CD 4011
17th/18th Century Italian Songs
High Voice, Volume 2 ....MMO CD 4013
Advanced Mezzo Soprano Solos ....MMO CD 4045
Beginning Mezzo Soprano Solos ...MMO CD 4043
Beginning Soprano Solos ....MMO CD 4041
BELLINI La Sonnambula: Scenes and Arias
for Soprano and Orchestra ....MMO CDG 4064
BELLINI Opera Scenes and Arias
for Soprano and Orchestra ....MMO CDG 4063
BRAHMS German Lieder - High Voice...........MMO CD 4005
DONIZETTI Soprano Arias with Orchestra..MMO CDG 4058
DVORAK and TCHAIKOVSKY
Soprano Arias with Orchestra........MMO CDG 4076
Everybody's Favorite Songs
High Voice, Volume 1 ....MMO CDG 4007
Everybody's Favorite Songs
High Voice, Volume 2 ....MMO CDG 4009
Famous Soprano Arias................MMO CDG 4015
French Arias For Soprano.............MMO CD 4029

French Opera Arias for Soprano
and Orchestra ....MMO CDG 4070
Intermediate Mezzo Soprano Solos................MMO CD 4044
Intermediate Soprano Solos............MMO CD 4042
Italian Arias For Soprano ....MMO CD 4028
MOZART Arias For Soprano ....MMO CDG 4026
MOZART Opera Arias for Soprano
and Orchestra, vol. I ....MMO CDG 4060
MOZART Opera Arias for Soprano
and Orchestra, vol. II ....MMO DG 4065
MOZART Opera Arias for Soprano
and Orchestra, vol. III...............MMO CDG 4087
Oratorio Arias For Soprano ....MMO CD 4030
PUCCINI Arias for Soprano
and Orchestra, vol. II ....MMO CDG 4079
PUCCINI Arias for Soprano
with Orchestra, vol. I ....MMO CDG 4053
SCHUBERT German Lieder
High Voice, Volume 1 ....MMO CDG 4001
SCHUBERT German Lieder
High Voice, Volume 2 ....MMO CDG 4003
SCHUBERT German Lieder
Low Voice, Volume 1 ....MMO CDG 4002
SCHUMANN German Lieder For High Voice..MMO CD 4024
Soprano Arias with Orchestra, vol. I...........MMO CDG 4052
Soprano Arias with Orchestra, vol. II ....MMO CDG 4054
STRAUSS German Lieder For High Voice ......MMO CD 4022
VERDI Arias For Soprano ....MMO CD 4027
VERDI Soprano Arias
with Orchestra, vol. I ....MMO CDG 4059
VERDI Soprano Arias
with Orchestra, vol. II ....MMO CDG 4072
WOLF German Lieder For High Voice ....MMO CD 4020

Vocal Tenor

Advanced Tenor Solos ....MMO CD 4049
Arias for Tenor and Orchestra
from the repertoire of Andrea Bocelli..........MMO CDG 4069
Beginning Tenor Solos ....MMO CD 4047
Famous Tenor Arias....................MMO CDG 4017
Intermediate Tenor Solos.................MMO CD 4048
Italian Tenor Arias with Orchestra ....MMO CDG 4057
Oratorio Arias For Tenor ....MMO CD 4032
PUCCINI Arias for Tenor
and Orchestra, vol. I ....MMO CDG 4061
Romantic Arias for Tenor & Orchestra ....MMO CDG 4085
VERDI Opera Arias for Tenor
and Orchestra ....MMO CDG 4067

Contents to these albums may be seen on our website at: www.musicminusone.com

A

And The World Goes 'Round - Kander & Ebb (2 CD Set) ....PSCDG 1513
Andrew Lloyd Webber ....PSCDG 1054
Andrew Lloyd Webber ....PSCDG 1130
Andrew Lloyd Webber (2 CD Set) ....PSCDG 1559
Andrew Lloyd Webber ....JTG 180
Annie ....PSCDG 1172
Annie Get Your Gun (2 CD Set) ....PSCDG 1186
Anything Goes ....PSCDG 1516
Austin Powers' Hits ....PSCDG 1433

B

Bee Gee Hits - Saturday Night Fever (F) ....PSCDG 1250
Best Little Whorehouse In Texas (F) ....PSCDG 1387
Best Of Broadway - Hollywood Sound Stage Orchestra ....PSCDG 6004
Best Of Broadway - Hollywood Sound Stage Orchestra ....PSCDG 6005
Best Of Broadway ....STCDG 121
Best Of Broadway ....JTG 128
Best Of Broadway & Films ....JTG 129
Big, Brass & Beautiful Broadway's Best ....PSCDG 1233
Bing Crosby Hits (F) ....PSCDG 1377
Boys On The Side (F) ....PSCDG 1191
Broadway Gems ....PSCDG 1448
Broadway Memories ....JTG 125
Broadway Hits for Soprano ....PSCDG 1341
Broadway Hits for Mezzo-Soprano ....PSCDG 1342
Broadway Hits for Alto Voice ....PSCDG 1343
Broadway Hits for Tenor Voice ....PSCDG 1344
Broadway Hits for Baritone ....PSCDG 1345
Broadway Hits for Bass ....PSCDG 1346
Broadway Duets ....PSCDG 1347
Broadway Men ....PSCDG 1348
Broadway Men ....JTG 160
Broadway Women ....PSCDG 1349
Broadway Women ....JTG 162
Bye Bye Birdie ....JTG 063

C

Camelot ....PSCDG 1173
Carousel ....PSCD 1180
Chess ....JTG 060

D

Disney's Broadway...PSCDG 1268
Disney New Movies ....JT 114
Disney Songs - Your Favorites ....PSCD 1198

E

Elvis In The Movies (F) ....PSCDG 1074
Escape Master - James Bond Themes (F) ....PSCDG 1263
Evita ....JTG 037
Evita (2 CD Set) ....PSCDG 1557

F

Fantasticks ....PSCDG 1182
Fiddler On The Roof (2 CD Set) ....PSCDG 1179
Full Monty, The - The Producers ....PRO 1

G

Gershwin/Feinstein ....JTG 052
Godspell ....PSCDG 1241
Grease (F) ....PSCDG 1196
Guys And Dolls ....PSCDG 1067

H

Harold Arlen Hits (F) ....PSCDG 1077
Harold Arlen Songbook ....JTG 130
Harry Warren Hits ....PSCDG 1530
Hello Dolly (2 CD Set)..PSCDG 1187

F = *Film* • PSCDG: *with Vocals* • JTG: *Just Tracks, Backgrounds only, no vocal*
ST: *Screen Tracks* • PSCD: *with vocals, no graphics*

J

Jekyll & Hyde .... PSCDG 1151
Jekyll & Hyde .... JTG 020
Jerome Kern .... PSCDG 1405
Jerome Kern Songs .... JTG 132
Jerry Herman Hits .... JTG 067
Jesus Christ Superstar (2 CD Set) .... PSCDG 1588
Jimmy McHugh Hits .... PSCDG 1517
Judy Garland Hits .... PSCDD 1285

K

King And I .... PSCDG 1178
Kurt Weill and Friends .... PSCDG 1529

L

La Cage Aux Folles - Mame - Mack & Mabel - Hello Dolly .... JTG 067
Let's Go To The Movies .... JTG 113
Lerner & Lowe Songs .... JTG 117
Les Miserables .... PSCDG 1350
Linda Eder Hits - Frank Wildhorn .... PSCDG 1488
Linda Eder Broadway and other hits .... JTG 198
Little Shop Of Horrors .... PSCDG 1400
Louis Armstrong & Jimmy Durante .... JTG 195

M

Mack & Mabel - Mame - La Cage Aux Folles - Hello Dolly .... JTG 067
Mame - La Cage Aux Folles - Mack & Mabel - Hello Dolly .... JTG 067
Mamma Mia .... PRO 2
Michel Legrand Hits (2 CD Set) .... PSCDG 1546
Miss Saigon .... PSCDG 1236
Mr. Holland's Opus .... PSCDG 1209
Music Man, The .... PSCDG 1183
My Fair Lady (2 CD Set) .... PSCDG 1174

N

Notting Hill Hits (F) .... PSCDG 1447

O

Oklahoma .... PSCDG 1175
Oliver (2 CD Set) .... PSCDG 1189

P

Pal Joey .... PSCDG 1527
Peter Pan, Wizard of Oz & Friends (F) .... PSCDG 1483
Phantom Of The Opera .... PSCDG 1185
Pippin .... JTG 049
Porgy And Bess .... PSCD 1181
Preacher's Wife .... PSCDG 1237
Preacher's Wife / Sister Act 2 .... JTG 120
Producers, The - The Full Monty .... PRO 1

R

Runaway Bride (F) .... PSCDG 1453

S

Saturday Night Fever .... PSCDG 1408
Scarlet Pimpernel (2 CD Set) .... PSCDG 1389
Scarlet Pimpernel .... PSCDG 1512
Scarlet Pimpernel .... JTG 020
Sensational Cinema Singles (F) .... PSCDG 1254
Showboat .... PSCD 1160
Smokey Joe's Café .... PSCDG 1197
Sound Of Music (2 CD Set) .... PSCD 1176
South Pacific .... PSCD 1177
Stephen Sondheim .... JTG 068
Sunset Boulevard .... PSCDG 1193

T

Thanks For The Memories - Bing,Bob and Fred .... JTG 124

W

Walt's World - Disney Films (F) .... PSCD 1246
Wizard Of Oz - Peter Pan - Animal Hit (F) .... JTG 111

Visit our two websites: www.musicminusone.com and www.pocketsongs.com

THE SUPERSCOPE PSD230

PROFESSIONAL XLR & 1/4"
MIC/LINE INPUTS/
MIX LEVEL
CONTROL

EASY-TO-USE TOP-PANEL
PLAY/NAVIGATION/PROGRAM
AND TONE/PITCH CONTROLS

VOCAL LEAD
REDUCTION
ANALOGUE OUTPUTS
DIGITAL OUTPUT
FOOT PEDAL INPUT

1/4" HEADPHONE
JACK

BACKLIT LCD SCREEN
WITH EASY-TO-READ DISPLAY

FRONT-PANEL
VOLUME AND TONE
CONTROLS

OPTIONAL RC300 NECK/WRIST REMOTE

OPTIONAL FT200 FOOT-PEDAL

SUPERSCOPE

The machine that musicians have dreamed about since the beginning of recorded sound, a portable, variable-speed and pitch CD player.

$**499**.00 *plus shipping (save $100.00)*
Full details on our website. See it now!

FINE TUNING - KEY CONTROL: *you can change key, maintain tempo, for 1 octave.* **TEMPO CONTROL:** *increase tempo 50% or reduce tempo 33% in 50 increments, without changing key.* **LEAD VOCAL REDUCTION - A-B PRACTICE LOOP:** *rehearse difficult parts and record your final results again and again. Remote control available. Fine tune the CD to your instrument.*

Music Minus One Price Schedule
Some Exceptions exist

All MMO Instrumental albums	$29.98 each
MMO 2 CD Sets	$34.98 each
MMO Piano Editions	$34.98 each
MMO 2 CD Set Piano Editions	$39.98 each
20th Century Piano Editions	$34.98 each
Gershwin, Glazunov, etc.	
Vocal Editions	$29.98 each
John Wustman, Piano Accompanist	
Opera with Orchestra Editions	$34.98 each
Rutgers Univ. Dictation Series	$98.50 each
Music Dictation & Ear Training (7 CD Set)	
Baermann Clarinet Methods	$49.98 each
MMO 3240 & 3241 (4 CD Sets)	
Broadway CDG's	$29.98 sugg. list price
Broadway 2 CDG Sets	$34.98 sugg. list price

Music Minus One
Pocket Songs
50 Executive Boulevard
Elmsford, New York 10523-1325
www.musicminusone.com
www.pocketsongs.com

PRSRT STD A
US POSTAGE
PAID
WHITE PLAINS, NY
PERMIT #7033